SUPER SANDCASTLE™
Animal Habitats

What Lives in the Ocean?

Oona Gaarder-Juntti

Consulting Editor, Diane Craig, M.A./Reading Specialist

ABDO
Publishing Company

Published by ABDO Publishing Company, 8000 West 78th Street, Edina, Minnesota 55439. Copyright © 2009 by Abdo Consulting Group, Inc. International copyrights reserved in all countries. No part of this book may be reproduced in any form without written permission from the publisher. Super SandCastle™ is a trademark and logo of ABDO Publishing Company.

Printed in the United States.

Credits
Editor: Liz Salzmann
Content Developer: Nancy Tuminelly
Cover and Interior Design and Production: Oona Gaarder-Juntti, Mighty Media
Illustration: Oona Gaarder-Juntti
Photo Credits: AbleStock, iStockphoto/Charles Babbitt/Robert Dant/Tatiana Mironenko, Cole Brandon/Darlyne A. Murawski/Peter Arnold Inc., ShutterStock

Library of Congress Cataloging-in-Publication Data

Gaarder-Juntti, Oona, 1979-

What lives in the ocean? / Oona Gaarder-Juntti.

  p. cm. -- (Animal habitats)

ISBN 978-1-60453-175-6

1. Marine animals--Juvenile literature. 2. Marine ecology--Juvenile literature. I. Title.

QL122.2.G23 2008

591.77--dc22

2008005478

Super SandCastle™ books are created by a team of professional educators, reading specialists, and content developers around five essential components— phonemic awareness, phonics, vocabulary, text comprehension, and fluency— to assist young readers as they develop reading skills and strategies and increase their general knowledge. All books are written, reviewed, and leveled for guided reading, early reading intervention, and Accelerated Reader® programs for use in shared, guided, and independent reading and writing activities to support a balanced approach to literacy instruction.

About SUPER SANDCASTLE™

Bigger Books for Emerging Readers

Grades K–4

Created for library, classroom, and at-home use, Super SandCastle™ books support and engage young readers as they develop and build literacy skills and will increase their general knowledge about the world around them. Super SandCastle™ books are part of SandCastle™, the leading PreK–3 imprint for emerging and beginning readers. Super SandCastle™ features a larger trim size for more reading fun.

Let Us Know
Super SandCastle™ would like to hear your stories about reading this book. What was your favorite page? Was there something hard that you needed help with? Share the ups and downs of learning to read. We want to hear from you! Send us an e-mail.

sandcastle@abdopublishing.com

Contact us for a complete list of SandCastle™, Super SandCastle™, and other nonfiction and fiction titles from ABDO Publishing Company.

www.abdopublishing.com • 8000 West 78th Street
Edina, MN 55439 • 800-800-1312 • 952-831-1632 fax

The ocean is a huge body of water. It covers 71 percent of the earth. Over 97 percent of the water on earth is in the ocean. Millions of different species live in the ocean.

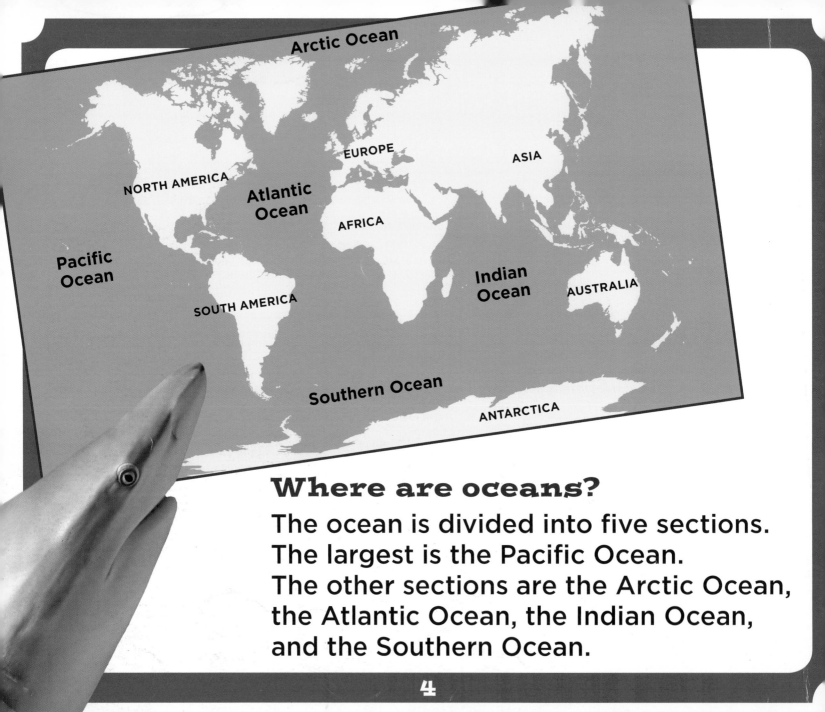

Where are oceans?

The ocean is divided into five sections.
The largest is the Pacific Ocean.
The other sections are the Arctic Ocean,
the Atlantic Ocean, the Indian Ocean,
and the Southern Ocean.

What does the ocean look like?

The ocean can be more than two miles deep in some places. There are three zones in the ocean.

Sunlight Zone (euphotic zone)

The sunlight zone is the top 250 feet of the ocean. It receives the most sunlight and 90 percent of all ocean animals live here.

Twilight Zone (disphotic zone)

The twilight zone is between 250 feet and 650 feet deep. Very little sunlight reaches this zone. Plants can't grow here. Squid, octopus, and mid-water jellyfish live here.

Midnight Zone (aphotic zone)

The rest of the ocean is the midnight zone. It is the coldest and darkest zone because no sunlight ever reaches there. Deep-sea angler fish and sea cucumbers live here.

Sea Cucumber

Animal class: Invertebrate
Location: Every ocean

Sea cucumbers live on the ocean floor. When threatened, a sea cucumber spits out its internal organs. This confuses predators. The sea cucumber's organs grow back later.

A sea cucumber has tentacles surrounding its mouth. The tentacles help it catch food floating in the water.

8

LEAFY SEA DRAGON

Animal class: Fish
Location: Indian Ocean

Leafy sea dragons are related to sea horses. They can't swim very fast. They rely on their leaf-like camouflage to hide them from predators.

A leafy sea dragon uses its tube-shaped mouth to suck up small sea creatures.

9

JELLYFISH

Animal class: Invertebrate
Location: Every ocean

Jellyfish have bell-shaped bodies and long, poisonous tentacles. They use their tentacles to grab and sting their prey. Jellyfish live for three to six months.

Jellyfish are 98 percent water. They don't have brains, hearts, eyes, ears, or bones.

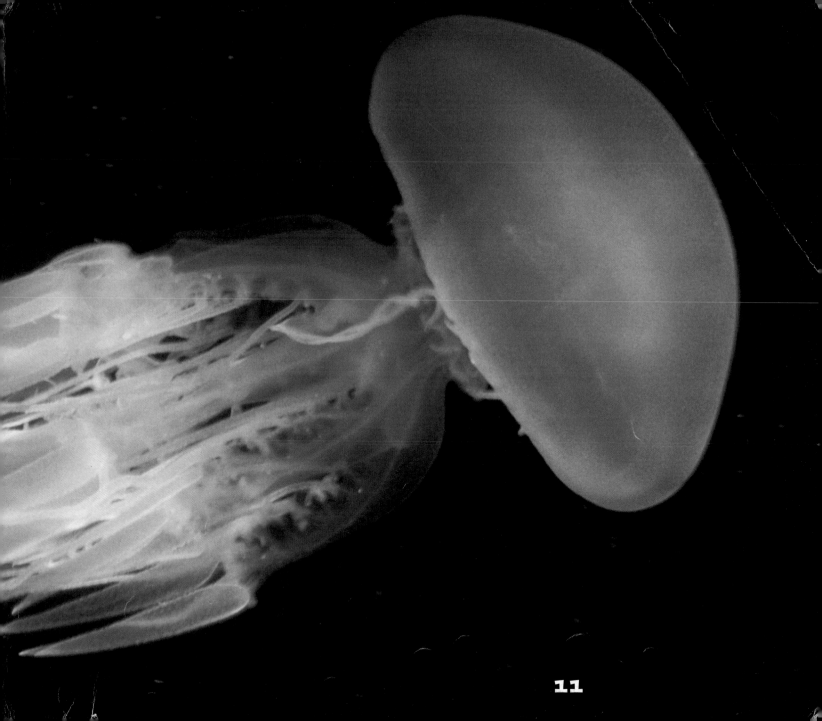

11

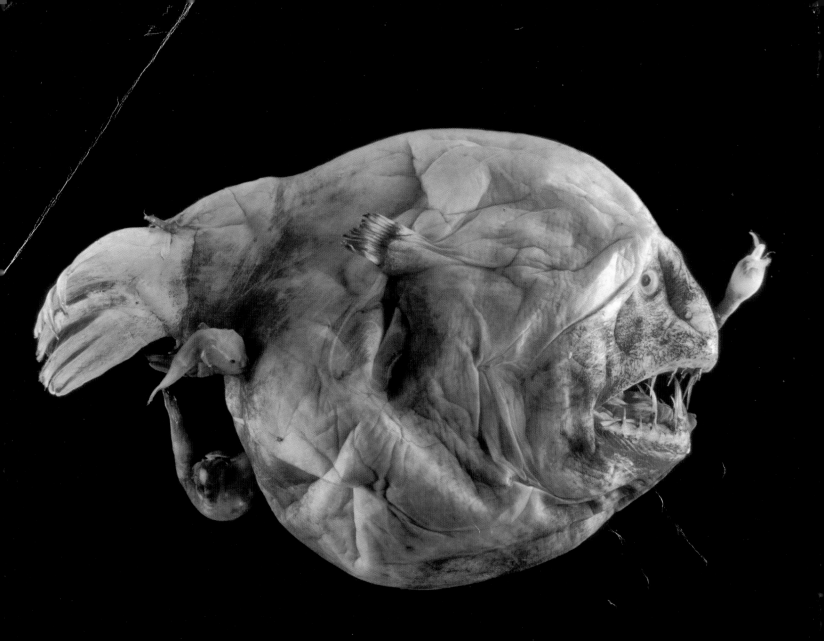

DEEP-SEA ANGLERFISH

Animal class: Fish
Location: Atlantic Ocean and Southern Ocean

Deep-sea anglerfish live in the deepest parts of the ocean where there is no light. The female has a spine sticking out of her head.

The spine on the female's head glows to attract prey.

HUMPHEAD WRASSE

Animal class: Fish
Location: Pacific Ocean and Indian Ocean

Humphead wrasses can grow up to seven feet long and weigh more than 400 pounds. They use their strong jaws and teeth to crush creatures that have shells.

Humphead wrasses can eat prey that is toxic to most other predators.

16

OCTOPUS

Animal class: Invertebrate
Location: Every ocean

Octopuses can change color to match their surroundings. When threatened by a predator, an octopus squirts out black ink. This helps it escape without being seen.

Octopuses have eight arms. The suction cups on their arms help them grab on to their prey.

DOLPHIN

Animal class: Mammal
Location: Pacific Ocean
and Atlantic Ocean

Dolphins are fast swimmers. They leap in and out of the water to breathe while swimming. A dolphin breathes through a blowhole on top of its head.

Dolphins can leap as high as 20 feet into the air.

GREAT WHITE SHARK

Animal class: Fish
Location: Every ocean

Great white sharks are the largest fish that catch and eat prey. They can grow up to 20 feet long and weigh up to 5,000 pounds. The great white shark has 3,000 teeth.

Great white sharks can swim up to 15 miles per hour. They can even jump out of the water to attack prey.

More Ocean Animals

Can you learn about these ocean animals?

auk

baleen whale

brown pelican

bubble coral

cuttlefish

elephant seal

giant squid

krill

lionfish

loggerhead sea turtle

manta ray

marlin

sea lion

sea otter

sea snake

swordfish

trumpetfish

walrus

zooplankton

Glossary

attract – to cause someone or something to come near.

camouflage – a method of hiding from sight by using a disguise or protective coloring to blend in to the surroundings.

female – being of the sex that can produce eggs or give birth. Mothers are female.

internal organ – a body part that is entirely inside the body, such as a heart or lung.

invertebrate – a creature that does not have a spine.

mammal – a warm-blooded animal that has hair and whose females produce milk to feed the young.

prey – an animal that is hunted or caught for food.

rely – to trust or depend on.

species – a group of related living beings.

suction cup – a flexible cup that sticks when the open end is pressed to a flat surface.

tentacle – a long, flexible limb on an invertebrate such as a jellyfish, octopus, or squid.

threatened – to feel frightened by something.

zone – an area that is set off for a specific use or purpose.